Destination Detectives

Australia

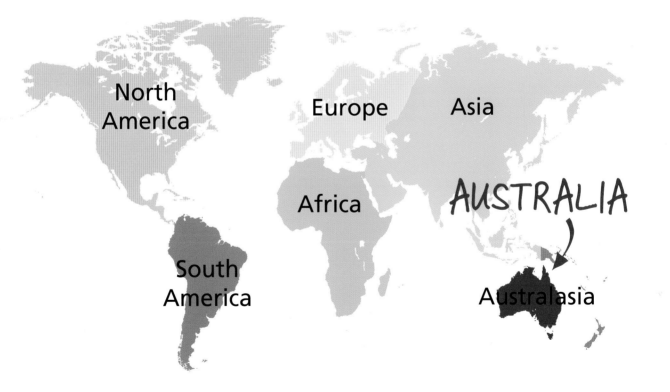

North
America

Europe

Asia

Africa

AUSTRALIA

South
America

Australasia

Miriam Lumb

Raintree

www.raintreepublishers.co.uk

Visit our website to find out more information about **Raintree** books.

To order:
☎ Phone 44 (0) 1865 888112
🗎 Send a fax to 44 (0) 1865 314091
💻 Visit the Raintree Bookshop at **www.raintreepublishers.co.uk** to browse our catalogue and order online.

Produced for Raintree by
White-Thomson Publishing Ltd,
Bridgewater Business Centre,
210 High Street, Lewes, BN7 2NH

First published in Great Britain by Raintree,
Halley Court, Jordan Hill, Oxford OX2 8EJ,
Part of Harcourt Education.
Raintree is a registered trademark of
Harcourt Education Ltd.

Editorial: Sonya Newland, Melanie Waldron,
and Lucy Beevor
Design: Gary Frost
Picture Research: Amy Sparks
Production: Chloe Bloom

Originated by Modern Age
Printed and bound in China
by South China Printing Company

10 digit ISBN 1406203122
13 digit ISBN 9781406203127
10 9 8 7 6 5 4 3 2 1
11 10 09 08 07 06

British Library Cataloguing in Publication Data
Lumb, Miriam
    Australia. - (Destination Detectives)
    1. Australia - Geography - Juvenile literature 2. Australia
    - Social life and customs - 21st century - Juvenile
    literature 3. Australia - Civilization - Juvenile literature
    I. Title
    994'.07

Acknowledgements
Alamy pp. 37 (Davo Blair); Bridgeman Art Library
pp. 30 (Private Collection); Corbis pp. 9 (Penny Tweddle),
16 (Penny Tweddle), 22 (Tim Wimborne/Reuters),
31 (Van Hasselt John), 38 (Van Hasselt John), 39 (Michael
& Patricia Fogden), 41 (David Callow/Reuters); istockphoto
pp. 7t, 13b; Photolibrary pp. 7b (Robert Harding Picture
Library Ltd), 10 (Robert Harding Picture Library Ltd),
11l (Robin Smith), 11r (Photolibrary.com Australia),
12 (Photolibrary.com Australia), 13t (Pacific Stock),
14 (Index Stock Imagery), 17 (Robert Harding Picture
Library Ltd), 18 (Photolibrary.com Australia), 19 (Robin
Smith), 20 (Pacific Stock), 21 (Photolibrary.com Australia),
24-25 (Brandx Pictures), 27 (Photolibrary.com Australia),
33 (Photolibrary.com Australia), 34r (Photolibrary.com
Australia), 35 (Photolibrary.com Australia), 36 (Index
Stock Imagery), 40 (Photolibrary.com Australia),
42-43 (Photolibrary.com Australia), 43 (Photolibrary.com
Australia); Popperfoto pp. 34l; TopFoto pp. 4-5, 15;
WTPix pp. 5t, 5m, 5b, 8, 23, 25, 28, 29, 32.

Cover photograph of Uluru reproduced with permission
of Photolibrary/Index Stock Imagery

Every effort has been made to contact copyright
holders of any material reproduced in this book.
Any omissions will be rectified in subsequent
printings if notice is given to the publishers.

Contents

Any words appearing in the text in bold, **like this,** are explained in the glossary. You can also look out for them in the Word Bank box at the bottom of each page.

Where in the world?

The southern continent

The name Australia comes from the Latin word *Australis*, which means "southern". Australia is the only country that is also a **continent**. It is the sixth-largest country in the world, but the smallest continent.

Bang! A starter gun shatters your dreams. *Go Go Go!* A dozen bodies break free from the heaving crowd. Feet beat. Sand sprays. Colourful caps bob up and down, racing to be the first to dive head-first into the sparkling blue ocean.

High-rise buildings tower over the beach where you stand, in the middle of an excited crowd. A breeze carries the sweet smell of barbequed onions and sausages. As you eagerly look to see where the smell is coming from, trying to work out where you are, the banner stretched across the starting line catches your eye: The Australian Surf Life Saving Championships. So you're in Australia. This is sure to be an adventure!

With 7,500 competitors in the Surf Life Saving Championships, only the Olympic Games has more participants.

➤

WORD BANK   continent one of the world's large land masses

Surf Life Saving Australia (SLSA)

The Australian Surf Life Saving Championships are held every year. Members of the SLSA compete against each other, and overseas competitors, in various events over three days.

The SLSA is an organization of volunteer lifeguards. It has 115,000 members, who patrol the beaches of Australia, making sure that swimmers and surfers are safe in the water. Since 1907, Australia's surf lifesavers have saved nearly half a million lives.
Surf lifesavers compete in events at club, regional, state, national, and international levels.

Survival tip
Surf lifesavers mark the safe areas to swim with red and yellow flags.

Find out later...

What is the most isolated city in the world?

Where is this modern transport system?

How do children have lessons in the **outback**?

5

About Australia

A tourist in the crowd has a guidebook to Australia. Inside is a map of the country. You can see that Australia is actually a huge island, with a few smaller islands off the coast. The country is made up of six **states** and two **territories**. Most of the main cities seem to be on the coast. You trace the coastline until you meet an X on the eastern side. You are on Queensland's Gold Coast. This is one of Australia's top tourist destinations.

Northern Territory
The territory's capital, Darwin, is Australia's sunniest city — averaging 8.5 hours of sunshine each day.

INDONESIA

PAPUA NEW GUINEA

INDIAN OCEAN

Darwin•

Gulf of Carpentaria

Coral Sea

Great

SOUTH PACIFIC OCEAN

Cairns•

Western Australia
Perth is thought to be the most isolated city in the world, thousands of kilometres from any other major city.

NORTHERN TERRITORY

Alice Springs•

Uluru ▲(Ayers Rock)

WESTERN AUSTRALIA

QUEENSLAND

Brisbane•✗

SOUTH AUSTRALIA

NEW SOUTH WALES

Perth•

Sydney

Canberra•

Adelaide•

Australian Capital Territory
The Government couldn't decide whether Melbourne or Sydney should be Australia's capital. Instead, the city of Canberra was built in the middle.

N
W   E
S

0   500 km
0   300 miles

Mount Gambier•

VICTORIA
Melbourne•

AUSTRALIAN CAPITAL TERRITORY

SOUTHERN OCEAN

TASMANIA

New South Wales
The design for Sydney's Opera House was based on a ship's sails.

WORD BANK   algae small water plants
democratic ruled by the people

South Australia
Algae causes the Blue Lake, near Mount Gambier in South Australia, to turn a dazzling shade of blue every November.

Australia at a glance

OFFICIAL NAME: Commonwealth of Australia

CAPITAL: Canberra

POPULATION: 20 million

SIZE: 7,686,850 square kilometres (2,968,010 square miles)

OFFICIAL LANGUAGE: English

CURRENCY: Australian Dollar (AUD)

GOVERNMENT: Democratic, with three levels of government – federal, state, and local

Victoria
Melbourne's famous tramway system covers 244 kilometres (152 miles), and has 450 trams.

states different areas that make some of their own laws
territories areas of the country outside the states

Climate & landscape

Weather hazards

Severe droughts are common in parts of Australia, and they can last several years. Even though Australia is the driest inhabited **continent**, floods caused by heavy rainfall are also common, especially along the east coast. Areas affected by floods can also be affected by droughts.

Here in Queensland, on the east coast of Australia, the weather is **sub-tropical**. Most of the rain falls during hot and humid summers. In winter, the temperature rarely drops below 13°C (55°F).

Further north, the weather is tropical and has two seasons. The "wet season" lasts from November to March, and the "dry season" is from April to October.

The south-east and south-west of Australia have temperate **climates,** which means they have warm summers and mild to cool winters. There are four distinct seasons:
- Spring – September, October, November
- Summer – December, January, February
- Autumn – March, April, May
- Winter – June, July, August

People enjoy the warm weather in Darwin. The intense heat here can drive people a little crazy – this is referred to as "going troppo"!

WORD BANK climate regular pattern of weather in an area
bush land that is not very developed

Changing seasons

Australia is in the southern **hemisphere**, so the seasons are at opposite times of year to countries like the United Kingdom and the United States, in the northern hemisphere. This means that Christmas and New Year's Eve fall in summer time.

In the desert areas of Australia, temperatures can be extreme. It can be very hot during the day and cold at night. To explore this vast country, you'll have to pack for all sorts of weather!

Canberra bushfires

In January 2003, after the worst drought ever in Australia, lightning strikes sparked 150 bushfires in New South Wales and the Australian Capital Territory. The fires burned for a week before strong winds spread them into the suburbs of Canberra. Around 500 houses were destroyed, and four people died.

Bushfires are a threat in many places across Australia.

hemisphere one half of Earth, divided by the **Equator**
tropical related to the tropics – the warmest parts of the world

9

Australia's landscape

Australia is one of the oldest land masses in the world. The north of the country has rainforests, bushland, and huge **plains**. There are snowfields in the south-east, and good farmland in the east, south, and south-west. Inland from the east coast is a row of mountains called the Great Dividing Range. On the other side of this lie the slopes and plains, and eventually the desert.

The island of Tasmania lies off the south-east coast of Australia. The island's west coast is very rugged, and the middle of Tasmania is mountainous. Because of this, most of the people live in the north and south-east of the island.

Mount Kosciuszko

Australia is the flattest of all the **continents**. The highest point on the **mainland** is Mount Kosciuszko, at 2,228 metres (7,208 feet). It stands at the southern end of the Great Dividing Range. This area is a popular ski resort in winter, and is used by campers and bushwalkers in the summer.

Fast fact
Australia has hundreds of lakes, but many of them are dry most of the time!

People come from all over Australia to enjoy skiing in the Great Dividing Range.

WORD BANK irrigation supplying the land with water using streams, pipes, or ditches
mainland main part of Australia, not the islands

Rivers

Rivers are one of Australia's most important resources. They provide towns and cities with drinking water, and farmers with water for **irrigation**. Dams and reservoirs store water for the dry season.

The Murray-Darling river system is the largest in Australia. It flows for 2,520 kilometres (1,566 miles) through Queensland, Victoria, New South Wales, and South Australia. The Murrumbidgee River forms part of this system, stretching 1,575 kilometres (979 miles).

These wildflowers in the desert are known as "yellow tops".

Desert wildflowers

Many of Australia's wildflowers grow in the desert, with their seeds buried deep underground. After heavy rains, the desert bursts into bloom with spectacular flowers of all shapes and colours.

The meeting of the Murray and Darling rivers in New South Wales.

plain large area of flat country

Regions of Australia

Slip – Slop – Slap

"Slip on a shirt; slop on sunscreen; slap on a hat." This is a common summer-time slogan that should be taken seriously. Australia has the highest rate of skin cancer in the world – the sun can burn your skin in minutes! Most primary schools only allow children to play outside if they wear a hat.

You can see from your map that Australia is a giant island – it does not border any other countries. It is surrounded by 60,000 kilometres (37,284 miles) of coast, including the coast of Tasmania. The capital cities of all the **states** and **territories** are on the coast, except Canberra.

With 7,000 beaches to choose from, and the warm weather, it is no surprise that beach culture is an important part of life in Australia. Summer holidays are often spent by the beach, and thousands of Australians and tourists visit the coast every year. Swimming, surfing, diving, snorkelling, fishing, and sailing are popular beach activities.

Fast fact
Four out of five Australians live within 50 kilometres (31 miles) of the coast.

Bondi Beach, near Sydney, is one of the most popular tourist destinations in Australia.

WORD BANK coral reef long line of coral, close to the surface of the sea

Sea life

The Great Barrier Reef is the largest **coral reef** in the world. It follows the coast of Queensland for nearly 2,000 kilometres (1,243 miles). Snorkelling or scuba diving are the best ways to see the extraordinary animals, shapes, and colours of the reef. The Great Barrier Reef is so large it can be seen from the moon!

There are 4,000 species of fish living in Australia's waters. About 80 percent of marine life in the southern Australian waters cannot be found anywhere else in the world.

A Great White Shark swims in the warm waters off Australia's coast.

Sharks

People often worry about shark attacks in Australia. Nearly half of the world's shark species are found in the seas around Australia. Even so, shark attacks are rare.

From overhead, you can see the Great Barrier Reef just below the surface of the water.

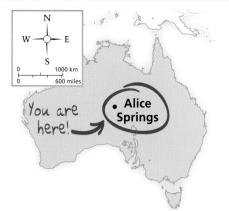

You are here!

Alice Springs

The desert

To find out more about the different regions of Australia, you decide to catch an aeroplane right to the middle of the country – Alice Springs. Your **Aboriginal** guide welcomes your tour group to the **outback**.

As you drive along, you realize that everywhere you look the landscape seems the same. There are huge stretches of land, with only occasional grasses and dry **creek beds**. The soil is rust-red and the sky is a deep blue.

The outback's icon

Uluru is the Aboriginal name for Ayers Rock, a huge sandstone rock covering 3.3 square kilometres (1.3 square miles) in the Northern Territory. Depending on the time of day and the weather, Uluru can change colour dramatically – from shades of blue to bright red!

Outback origins

The word "outback" came from the expression "out back of Bourke". Bourke is a place in the north of New South Wales, on the edge of the desert.

Uluru is a sacred site for the **indigenous** Aboriginal people of Australia.

➤

WORD BANK   **Aboriginal** describes a person whose ancestors were the first to live in Australia
creek bed bottom of a small stream of water

Australia's outback

Passing through a settlement, Aboriginal children wave to your guide. He explains that just over two percent of Australia's population are Aboriginal or **Torres Strait Islanders**. Two-thirds of these live in **rural** or remote areas.

It is very hot, and you are glad to stop at a waterhole, to have a splash around and to look at ancient Aboriginal rock art in nearby caves. Traditional bread called damper is cooked over an open fire for dinner – it is delicious! As you lie down, your guide points out five bright stars. Together these are known as the Southern Cross, and these are the stars that are shown on the Australian flag.

Recipe for damper

Mix together 2 cups of self-raising flour, 1/2 teaspoon of salt, and 2 teaspoons of sugar. Add 3 tablespoons of butter until crumbs form, then a cup of milk to make dough. Knead lightly. Shape into a round loaf, brush with milk, and bake at 190°C (373°F) for 35 minutes, until the loaf makes a hollow sound when tapped.

Aboriginal children attend schools in the Australian outback.

indigenous originally from a particular country
outback remote regions of Australia

Nearly all the world's best **opals** are mined in Australia. Coober Pedy is an opal-mining town in the South Australian outback. Most of the 3,500 people there live in comfortable homes built underground. These are called "dug-outs". Living underground provides shelter from the extreme heat – temperatures can reach 50°C (122°F) in this part of Australia.

Cattle stations in the outback can be up to 500,000 hectares (1,235,527 acres).

Farming

Most of Australia's money comes from farming and mining. **Agricultural** land covers about 60 percent of the country. Much of this is dry grazing land, and only 10 percent is used to grow crops. Dairy cattle farming is common in the southern **states,** especially Victoria.

Australian farms are usually family businesses. The number of farming families is decreasing and the size of farms is increasing. Many modern farmers need to find extra work away from the farm to make more money.

Mineral wealth

Australia has a lot of minerals, and is the world's top producer of **bauxite,** diamonds, and lead.

WORD BANK agricultural to do with farming
bauxite mineral that aluminium is made from

Living in remote Australia

As you continue your journey through the **outback**, your guide tells you about his time working as a "jackeroo" on a remote cattle station, learning how to brand and tag cattle, and helping to look after the property. Helicopters are often used to round up cattle because the cattle stations are so big!

People who live in the Australian outback are often hundreds of kilometres from emergency services. The Royal Flying Doctor Service is an organization that provides medical aid to remote areas. It has aeroplanes that operate as air ambulances.

Fast fact
Australia's top agricultural **exports** are cattle, wheat, wool, dairy products, and fruit.

The Royal Flying Doctor Service started in 1928. Today, it has 36 aircraft that help people all over Australia.

Turn those taps off!
The Government limits the amount of water people can use in times of drought. They can only water their gardens on certain days, and they must use a bucket and sponge instead of a hose to wash their cars. Water Restriction Patrols can fine anyone who breaks these rules.

export something that is sold to another country
opal mineral used as a gemstone – often to make jewellery

Wildlife

Hundreds of species of birds and animals can be found all over Australia – even in the hot, dry **outback**. Emus are birds as tall as humans. They can't fly, but they can run at speeds of up to 45 kilometres (28 miles) per hour! Nicknamed "Laughing Jackasses", Kookaburra birds are famous for their distinctive call, which sounds a bit like a human laugh.

Koalas often sleep for 20 hours a day. Platypus and echidna are the only egg-laying **mammals** in the world. The platypus can eat its own body weight in food in a 24-hour period!

The coat of arms

The official symbol of the Australian Government is a coat of arms. It is a shield, held by a kangaroo and an emu. It contains the badges of the six **states**.

Australia's native floral symbol, wattle, appears behind the kangaroo and the emu.
▶

Unusual animals

Over 80 percent of Australia's mammals and reptiles cannot be found anywhere else in the world. This is also true of most of the fish and almost half the birds!

AUSTRALIA

WORD BANK　　**endangered** in danger of disappearing altogether
mammal animal that gives birth to live babies

Other animals

The saltwater crocodile is the world's largest **reptile**. It can grow to up to 7 metres (23 feet) in length.

In addition to the kangaroos that live on land, there are species of **tropical** kangaroos that live in trees. There are also snakes, spiders, fairy penguins, and box jellyfish – whose sting can kill you.

Survival tip

Although Australia has a reputation for dangerous wildlife, it is unlikely you will come across any dangerous animals. Most of them are more scared of you than you are of them.

Going, going, gone...

Australia has more **endangered** species than any other **continent**. The number of bilbies, an animal that looks a bit like a rabbit, has been drastically reduced by foxes and fires. They used to be found across 70 percent of Australia's **mainland**, but now there are only a few left in Western Australia, the Northern Territory, and Queensland.

Kookaburras are most common in eastern parts of Australia.

---

reptile animal that has scaly skin and lays eggs

Gum trees

Eucalyptus trees, commonly known as gum trees, can be found all over Australia. There are over 700 species of the tree. Gum trees are well adapted to survive droughts, floods, and bushfires. The leaves can be used as a musical instrument by blowing air through them, placed firmly against the lower lip and lightly against the upper lip.

Plants

Australia's plants and flowers are the most varied in the world. They have had to adapt to many different landscapes, including **tropical** rainforests, stony deserts, mountains, and sandy areas. Because of this, plants have developed with special features that allow them to grow well in the different environments.

When Europeans first arrived in Australia, they replaced a lot of the native Australian plants with European ones. They also cleared much of the land for **pasture**. Today, Australians take a great interest in native plants. They are now popular in home gardens as well as public parks and gardens. National Parks, forests, and wilderness areas have been created to help protect Australia's natural plants and wildlife.

The shoots and leaves of gum trees are the only food that koalas eat.

WORD BANK   emblem object or picture that represents an organization or an idea

Australia's national emblem

The acacia, known as "wattle", is the national **emblem** of Australia. Wattle has large fluffy, yellow, sweet-smelling flower heads. Each of these is a bunch of many tiny flowers. Lots of Australians grow wattle trees in their gardens because of their sweet smell and pretty flowers.

Australia's national flower, wattle.

Fast fact
There are around 25,000 plants native to Australia.

Getting around

Australia is a huge country, and seeing all the different regions can involve travelling great distances. Travelling by plane is a good option if you don't have a lot of time. There are nearly 450 airports across Australia.

Long-distance trains

There are amazing train journeys across Australia. The Ghan train runs on the longest north-to-south rail-track in the world. It has recently been extended to stretch across the entire **continent**, from Adelaide to Darwin! There is also the Indian Pacific train, travelling from Sydney all the way to Perth, across the Nullabor Plain. The journey takes three days.

The Ghan train

The Ghan train is named after Afghan camel trains, which covered the same route, between Oodnadatta in South Australia and Alice Springs, before the railway lines were built. A series of camels carried goods and passengers along the track.

The Ghan train speeds through Australia's **outback**.

Bus journeys

Interstate bus tickets are affordable. You can buy passes to last a certain amount of time or distance. Remember that cities that look close together on a map, such as Melbourne and Sydney, will still take 12 hours to travel between by bus!

Australian cities have modern transport systems. These include trains, buses, ferries, and trams. Cars are the main form of transport, and most Australian families own at least one car.

Truck traffic
Australia has the highest use of trucks in the world. Trucks are the main way that goods are transported long distances.

The monorail transport system in Sydney.

The Ute
The world's most popular vehicle is an Australian invention. The utility truck – known as the "Ute" – had its beginnings in Gippsland, Victoria. In 1933, a pig farmer's wife came up with the idea for a vehicle that could "take the family to church on Sunday, and the pigs to town on a Monday". The first Ute was produced a year later.

Australian cities

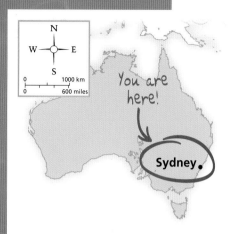

N
W   E
S

0   1000 km
0   600 miles

You are here!

Sydney

Now that you have seen the **outback**, it's time to find out more about Australia's cities, so you fly to Sydney, the capital of New South Wales.

One of the first things you see is the huge Sydney Harbour Bridge. You can actually climb to the top of the bridge – securely fastened by a harness. The views from the top are amazing. It is possible to see ferries, cruise boats, and sailing boats gliding across the glittering harbour. Trains, buses, cars, cyclists, and pedestrians criss-cross the bridge below. The Sydney Opera House and Darling Harbour look spectacular against the backdrop of the city and the sprawl of Sydney's suburbs.

The working week

Australians used to be limited to working for only 40 hours a week. Today, however, many people work much longer hours. Two million Australians work more than 50 hours a week.

The world-famous Sydney Opera House sits on the edge of the harbour, by the bridge.

▶

Bustling Sydney

Sydney is a busy and thriving city, and it is often mistaken for Australia's capital. The people who live here sometimes call themselves "Sydneysiders". You watch people rush among the high-rise office blocks, talking on their mobile phones, running for taxis, and working on laptops in cafés. Convenience stores, dotted between malls and department stores, advertise 24-hour opening times. It is a busy and exciting city.

Sydney's business district has many modern high-rise office blocks.

Sydney Harbour Bridge

The Sydney Harbour Bridge took eight years to build and was opened in 1932. It took 30,000 litres (6,600 gallons) of paint to cover it all. It is sometimes nicknamed the "coathanger" because of its shape.

Sydney suburbs

In Sydney's suburbs you notice that most houses are single-storey, detached, and have fences and a small garden. The house you are staying in has a large back yard – big enough for a swimming pool and a pet dog. After the evening meal, the family shows you photo albums of holidays in other Australian cities.

Perth

Perth, the capital of Western Australia, is famous for its Botanic Gardens in Kings Park. Here you can see 8,000 varieties of wildflower that cannot be found anywhere else in the world. The annual Wildflower Festival attracts thousands of visitors from around the world.

Change your clocks!

When travelling from city to city, you need to remember there are three time zones in Australia:

Eastern Standard Time
- New South Wales
- Victoria
- Queensland
- Tasmania
- ACT
11.00 a.m.

Central Standard Time
- South Australia
- Northern Territory
10.30 a.m.

Western Standard Time
- Western Australia
9.00 a.m.

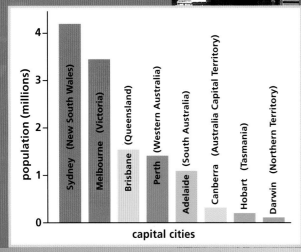

The modern, high-rise skyline of Western Australia's capital, Perth. ▼

26

Adelaide

Adelaide, the capital of South Australia, is surrounded by parklands. You can take a ride on paddleboats on the River Torrens or view the largest collection of Australian **Aboriginal** pieces in the world at the museum here.

Darwin

Darwin is the capital of the Northern Territory. Darwin was completely rebuilt after Cyclone Tracey destroyed the city on Christmas Eve in 1974. It is now a popular destination for backpackers.

Hobart

Hobart is the southernmost state capital in Australia, located in the south of the island of Tasmania. Hobart lies on the banks of the Derwent River, and Mount Wellington rises above it.

City living

Australia is one of the most highly urbanized countries in the world. This means that most of its population lives in the cities. The most densely populated areas are the east and south-east coasts.

Many cities have lakes, where people swim and ride in paddleboats.

City schooling

In Australia, children are required to attend school until the age of fifteen or sixteen, depending on which **state** they live in. Primary school usually lasts from age five to twelve and secondary school from age twelve to seventeen. Nearly 80 percent of children finish their final year of high school.

There are both private and public schools in Australia. Both types of school receive money from the Government, but you also have to pay fees to go to a private school. Private schools are often religious. Schools are **co-educational** or single sex.

Australia is a popular destination for international students, particularly from Asia. There are more than 165,000 overseas students studying in the country at any one time.

A sign by the side of the road advertising a grammar school in Queensland.

Unusual place names

Cadibarrawirracanna: A salt lake east of Coober Pedy, South Australia

Dead Dog Flat: Near Mount Garnet, Queensland

Mummarraboogungo-orangil: A large swamp near Duaringa, Queensland

TOWNSVILLE GRAMMAR SCHOOL

OPENING DOORS SINCE 1888

EDUCATING YOUTH IN NORTH QUEENSLAND

WORD BANK co-educational schools where boys and girls are taught together

Language

You have noticed that accents vary slightly from state to state, and there are phrases and language styles adopted by Australians that have given the English language a unique touch. One example of this is that Australians often shorten their words. University becomes uni, barbeque becomes barbie, afternoon is arvo, and vegetables are veggies.

Until the arrival of Europeans in Australia in the 18th century, there were about 700 **Aboriginal** languages and **dialects** spoken across Australia. Now there are fewer than 250, and most of them are no longer spoken as a first language. You decide to find out a bit more about Australia's history and other effects the Europeans had on the **indigenous** people.

Schools of the Air

To help students who live in remote areas, where there are no schools, the Australian Government created "Schools of the Air". Lessons and homework are sent by mail, and two-way radios are used to communicate. Now most pupils also use the Internet and email.

Children who live in **outback** areas work at home and communicate with their teachers by radio.

dialect form of language spoken in a particular area or by a particular group

A bit of history

Aboriginal Australians had lived in Australia for more than 50,000 years before European settlers arrived. Living as hunters and gatherers, they had a very close and respectful relationship with the land. Rather than owning it, they believed that they were another part of nature.

European settlement

The first recorded foreign explorers to land in Australia were the Dutch in 1606, followed by the British in 1688. In 1770, Captain James Cook arrived on the east coast of Australia and claimed the land for the United Kingdom. When the new settlers arrived, they gave little consideration to the **indigenous** people.

A fitting punishment?

Some of the convicts sent to Australia had committed crimes such as stealing a loaf of bread or opening a letter addressed to someone else. For this, they were forced to go and live on the other side of the world. Many never saw their homes or families again.

A group of prisoners in Sydney, shortly after the British arrived there.

WORD BANK   Torres Strait Islander someone who comes from this part of Queensland

At first, the British used Australia as a place to send people who had committed crimes. Life for these convicts was very difficult in Australia, as there was not much fresh food. They had to learn how to grow crops in the dry soil, and how to trade with the Aboriginals. Soon, though, people chose to move to Australia, as they were offered a free voyage and their own land when they arrived. These people were known as "free settlers".

Early Australian peoples

The Torres Strait Islands lie in the body of water that separates the Australian **mainland** from Papua New Guinea. **Torres Strait Islanders** live there and on the mainland, mostly in Townsville and Cairns. They have a separate culture and identity to Aboriginal Australians. Their lifestyle and culture is based on the sea.

The people who live on the Torres Strait Islands are proud of their native customs and beliefs.

Multicultural Australia

Over the years, people from other countries also settled in Australia, which is why Australia is still a **multicultural** country. These people left their homelands for many reasons.

In the 1850s, gold was discovered in Australia, and more than 26,000 Chinese people travelled there in the hope of making their fortunes.

When World War II ended in 1945, many Italians, Greeks, and northern Europeans arrived in Australia looking for work.

After the Vietnam War ended in the mid-1970s, many Vietnamese who had supported the losing side fled their country. Those **refugees** who arrived in Australia by boat became known as "boat people". Today, Vietnamese make up the third-largest **ethnic group** in Australia. There are around 160,000 Vietnamese living in Australia.

Australian facts

- One in four Australians was born in another country.
- About 40 percent of Australians have a parent born outside Australia.
- There are more than 100 ethnic groups.
- An estimated 240 languages are spoken in Australia.
- Since 1945, over six million people from 200 countries have settled here.
- More than 15 percent of the population speaks a language other than English.

► The Asian influence can be seen in many places across Australia. This is an Asian food shop in Sydney.

WORD BANK ethnic group people who share a culture or nationality
multicultural country that has people from many different cultures

Australia today

Australia is run by its own government and parliament. Officially, though, Queen Elizabeth II of the United Kingdom is the head of state. The Queen is represented in Australia by a Governor-General. Australia is often referred to as a "melting pot" because there are so many different cultures living together.

Fast fact
New Zealanders are the largest ethnic group in Australia.

The Gold Rush

In the 1850s, many people rushed to New South Wales when gold was discovered there. This meant that other towns and cities suffered. To keep people living in the **state** of Victoria, the Government there offered a reward for the first person to find gold close to Melbourne. It was not long before gold was found here and in other parts of Australia.

Children from different ethnic groups in Australia hold up the **Aboriginal** flag.

Australian culture

Cathy Freeman

Cathy Freeman is one of the most famous Australian athletes. She has won many medals at an international level. The highlight of her career came at the Sydney 2000 Olympics, when she won gold in the 400 metres. In 1990, Cathy was named Young Australian of the Year and in 1998 she was Australian of the Year.

You take a trip to Melbourne, the home of Australian Rules Football, to attend a pre-season match. This sport is known as "Aussie Rules". It developed from Gaelic football, which is played in Ireland, and an **Aboriginal** game called mangrook, which involved kicking and high-catching a ball. The match is very exciting – you can see why it is Australia's most popular spectator sport.

A huge crowd gathers at the stadium in Perth to watch a game of Aussie Rules Football.

Cathy Freeman, gold medallist at the Sydney Olympics.

A sporting nation

Australians take their sport very seriously. Even though the population is only around 20 million, Australia is one of the most successful sporting nations in the world. In the Sydney 2000 Olympic Games, Australia collected 58 medals – only one less than China, which has a population of 1.3 billion!

You can see that even if you are not into playing a sport, being a spectator is just as important and fun. After news and current affairs, sport has the highest television ratings. Netball, Rugby Union and Rugby League, cricket, swimming, tennis, and cycling are also popular Australian sports.

Winter sports

Tourists are often surprised that skiing and snowboarding are popular winter activities in Australia. There are world-class ski resorts in the **states** of Victoria and New South Wales.

The Todd River Regatta

The Todd River Regatta is held annually in Alice Springs, in the Northern Territory. This is not a normal boat race though – it takes place in a river with no water! Competitors run along the river bed in home-made boats, with their feet sticking out of the bottom. The day ends with a water-cannon fight!

Competitors begin the race at the Todd River Regatta.

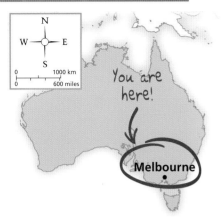

You are here!

Melbourne

Eating out

You are really hungry after the match! Your friends take you to dinner in Lygon Street in the north of Melbourne – this street is famous for its many Italian restaurants and outdoor dining.

Because of the large number of European **immigrants**, Greek, Italian, and other European styles of cooking are popular in Australia. Indian and Southeast Asian cooking styles are also common. Chinese restaurants can be found in many places, and you will find Indian, Japanese, Thai, and Vietnamese restaurants in the larger cities. Eating out in cafés and restaurants, often sitting outdoors, is a popular leisure activity.

The Aussie barbeque

The weather is usually warm in Australia, so it is common to eat outside, especially for a special event with family or friends. Meat and vegetables are often cooked on a barbeque. Public parks, backyards, and the beach are popular spots for a barbeque or picnic.

The warm weather makes eating outdoors a popular pastime in Australia.

WORD BANK   immigrant person who has moved from one country to another

Eating at home

Evening meals at home are as varied as the people who eat them. Many households still prefer the English tradition of meat – beef is the most popular – and vegetables.

The different **climates** in Australia produce a wide range of fresh ingredients all year round, from **tropical** fruits in the north to citrus fruits in the south. Because it is surrounded by water, lots of fresh fish and seafood is available in Australia.

Fast fact

Popular fast food in Australia includes meat pies and pasties (meat and vegetables wrapped in flaky pastry), with a flavoured milk.

Bush tucker

Bush tucker is the name given to the native herbs, spices, fruits, vegetables, animals, birds, reptiles, and insects that can be eaten. **Aboriginals** survived on bush tucker for thousands of years. Today, bush tucker is still available. For example, you can buy wattle-seed ice cream, and Kangaroo, wallaby, emu, and crocodile are served at some speciality restaurants.

A selection of traditional bush tucker.

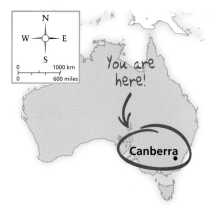

Canberra

The arts in Australia

Your journey round Australia would not be complete without a visit to Canberra, the nation's capital. The National Gallery of Australia is here, which gives you all sorts of information about Australian arts and culture.

Performing arts

Each **state** has its own major theatre company and symphony orchestra, in addition to smaller but well-known performing-arts groups. Australia also has a national opera company – the Australian Opera, and a national ballet company – the Australian Ballet.

The Australian capital

Canberra, the carefully planned capital of Australia, is nearly 100 years old and has a population of 320,000. The name "Canberra" is thought to have come from the **Aboriginal** word *Kamberra*, which means "meeting place". Australia's Parliament House is located here.

Indigenous art

Indigenous Australian art is currently one of the most celebrated art movements in the world, and is displayed in galleries from London to New York.

Indigenous dance company Bangarra combines traditional and modern dance forms.

Australian music has many successful acts. Among the best-known are Delta Goodrem, INXS, AC/DC, Little River Band, and Kylie Minogue. The national youth radio station, Triple J, promotes new Australian acts.

Each year, 40,000 Australian school students compete in the Rock Eisteddfod Challenge. They each perform an eight-minute dance, drama, and design spectacular, and compete against other schools for lots of prizes.

Australia produces its own distinctive style of documentaries and film. Well-known Australian actors include Nicole Kidman, Mel Gibson, Russell Crowe, and Cate Blanchett. Going to the cinema is one of the most popular pastimes in Australia.

Early ventures in film

In 1906, Australia produced one of the world's first feature films – *Story of the Kelly Gang*, about the famous bush ranger, Ned Kelly. There have been several films made about Ned Kelly since then.

"Dot painting" is a traditional technique used by Aboriginal Australians.

Come Out!

Come Out is the world's biggest arts festival for young people. It is held in South Australia every two years. Come Out has performances, exhibitions, arts events, and all kinds of creative activities.

National days

Australia Day, celebrated on 26 January, commemorates the arrival of eleven ships – called the first fleet – on the east coast of Australia in 1788. On this day the commander of the ship, Captain Arthur Phillip, established the first European settlement in the area.

ANZAC Day is celebrated on 25 April. It commemorates the landing at Gallipoli in Turkey of the Australian and New Zealand Army Corps (ANZACs) during World War I. More than 8,700 Australians were killed. Services and marches are held all over the country to remember this event.

Ships enter Sydney Harbour during the Australia Day celebrations.

Adelaide Festival of Arts

The Adelaide Festival of Arts is held in Adelaide every two years. The Adelaide Fringe Festival is held at the same time. This is Australia's biggest arts festival, and the second-biggest fringe festival in the world. You can see comedy, theatre, dance, cabaret, street theatre, film, and much more!

Other events

The Arafura Games are held in Darwin every two years. The Games are an international sporting competition for developing athletes of the Asia-Pacific region. The Sydney to Hobart Yacht Race starts the day after Christmas and is a huge spectacle as it leaves from Sydney Harbour.

The race that stops a nation

The Melbourne Cup is a horse-race held on the first Tuesday of November every year. Shops close and people stop what they are doing to watch the race on television.

In 2005, Makybe Diva became the first horse to win three Melbourne Cups in a row.

Stay or go?

You have seen a lot of Australia, but there is still so much left to see and do. You visit an Information Centre to see what else is on offer.

Still to see

Kangaroo Island is the place to meet Australia's wildlife in the wild. Wallabies, goannas, koalas, kangaroos, and echidnas all live on the island. You can reach Kangaroo Island by ferry or aeroplane.

A growing industry

In 2004, over five million tourists visited Australia. The majority came from New Zealand, Japan, and the United Kingdom. Tourism is one of the largest and fastest-growing industries in Australia.

Cradle Mountain and its lake in Tasmania.

WORD BANK   alpine relating to high mountains

Cradle Mountain in Tasmania is in a World Heritage Listed Area surrounded by rainforests, **alpine heathlands**, icy streams, and glacial lakes. It takes eight hours to walk to the top and back – but it's worth it!

The Kimberleys, in Western Australia, are a rugged wilderness landscape – famous for Cable Beach in Broome, one of the world's most stunning beaches. Here, you can take a camel ride as the sun sets.

You can bushwalk through the dramatic landscape of the Flinders Ranges in South Australia, swim with dolphins in Monkey Mia, or drive the Great Ocean Road on Victoria's coast.

Big things!

Don't be surprised if you come across an oversize banana towering over you in Coffs Harbour. Many Australian towns have huge model structures that you can often walk through or climb on! Other "Big Things" include the Big Rocking Horse in Gumeracha, in the Adelaide Hills, the Big Lobster in Kingston, South Australia, and the Big Penguin in Tasmania!

There are many giant statues all over Australia. This is the Golden Guitar in New South Wales.

heathland open land covered in rough grass

Find out more

World Wide Web

If you want to find out more about Australia, you can search the Internet using keywords such as these:

- Australia
- Sydney
- Great Barrier Reef
- Aboriginal

You can also find your own keywords by using headings or words from this book. Try using a search directory such as www.google.co.uk.

Films

Strictly Ballroom
A love story centred round a ballroom-dancing competition

Rabbit-Proof Fence
Based on the true story of three young **Aboriginal** girls who are separated from their family.

Destination Detectives can find out more about Australia by using the books and websites listed below.

The Australian Embassy

The Australian Embassy in your own country has lots of information about Australia. You can find out about the different states, the best times to visit, special events, and all about Australian culture.

The Australian Embassy website can be found at: http://australia.embassyhomepage.com/

Further reading

Countries of the World: Australia, Robert Prosser (Evans Brothers, 2004)
Explorers Wanted: In the Outback, Simon Chapman (Egmont Books, 2005)
Letters from Around the World: Australia, Margot Richardson (Cherrytree Books, 2004)
Nations of the World: Australia, Robert Darlington (Raintree, 2004)
Take Your Camera: Australia, Ted Park (Raintree, 2004)

Timeline

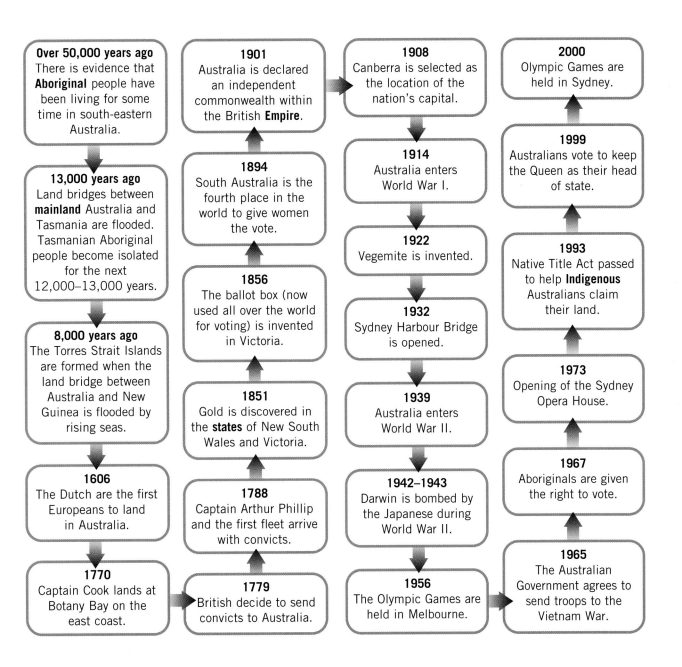

Over 50,000 years ago
There is evidence that **Aboriginal** people have been living for some time in south-eastern Australia.

13,000 years ago
Land bridges between **mainland** Australia and Tasmania are flooded. Tasmanian Aboriginal people become isolated for the next 12,000–13,000 years.

8,000 years ago
The Torres Strait Islands are formed when the land bridge between Australia and New Guinea is flooded by rising seas.

1606
The Dutch are the first Europeans to land in Australia.

1770
Captain Cook lands at Botany Bay on the east coast.

1779
British decide to send convicts to Australia.

1788
Captain Arthur Phillip and the first fleet arrive with convicts.

1851
Gold is discovered in the **states** of New South Wales and Victoria.

1856
The ballot box (now used all over the world for voting) is invented in Victoria.

1894
South Australia is the fourth place in the world to give women the vote.

1901
Australia is declared an independent commonwealth within the British **Empire**.

1908
Canberra is selected as the location of the nation's capital.

1914
Australia enters World War I.

1922
Vegemite is invented.

1932
Sydney Harbour Bridge is opened.

1939
Australia enters World War II.

1942–1943
Darwin is bombed by the Japanese during World War II.

1956
The Olympic Games are held in Melbourne.

1965
The Australian Government agrees to send troops to the Vietnam War.

1967
Aboriginals are given the right to vote.

1973
Opening of the Sydney Opera House.

1993
Native Title Act passed to help **Indigenous** Australians claim their land.

1999
Australians vote to keep the Queen as their head of state.

2000
Olympic Games are held in Sydney.

Australia – facts & figures

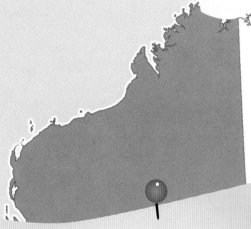

Australia's flag has six white stars on a blue background, and the UK flag in the left-hand corner. The Union Jack represents Australia's link to the UK. The large Commonwealth Star beneath it stands for all the states and territories. The five smaller stars are the Southern Cross, a constellation visible from all over Australia.

Technology boom

- Telephone lines: 10.8 million.
- Mobile phones: 14.3 million.
- Internet country code: .au.
- 42 percent of Australians have recently used a personal computer at home.

People and places

- Population: 20 million.
- Life expectancy: Male – 77 (Indigenous Australians – 59); Female – 83 (Indigenous Australian – 65).
- The largest lake in Australia is Lake Eyre, measuring 8,885 square kilometres (3,420 square miles). It is usually dry.

National anthem

- Australia's national anthem, Advance Australia Fair, is a revised version of a late nineteenth-century patriotic song.

Glossary

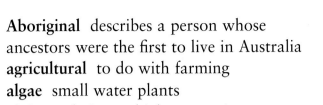

Aboriginal describes a person whose ancestors were the first to live in Australia

agricultural to do with farming

algae small water plants

alpine relating to high mountains

bauxite mineral that aluminium is made from

climate regular pattern of weather in an area

co-educational schools where boys and girls are taught together

continent one of the world's large land masses

coral reef long line of coral, close to the surface of the sea

creek bed bottom of a small stream of water

democratic ruled by the people

dialect form of language spoken in a particular area or by a particular group

emblem object or picture that represents an organization or an idea

empire group of countries under one ruler

endangered in danger of disappearing altogether

Equator imaginary line around the middle of Earth

ethnic group people who share a culture or nationality

export something that is sold to another country

heathland open land covered in rough grass

hemisphere one half of Earth, divided by the Equator

immigrant person who has moved from one country to another

indigenous originally from a particular country

irrigation supplying the land with water using streams, pipes, or ditches

mainland main part of Australia, not the islands

mammal animal that gives birth to live babies

multicultural country that has people from many different cultures

opal mineral used as a gemstone – often to make jewellery

outback remote regions of Australia

pasture land where farm animals graze

plain large area of flat country

refugee person who has been forced to leave his or her own country

reptile animal that has scaly skin and lays eggs

rural relating to the countryside

subtropical refers to a climate that is warm to hot in the summer and mild in winter

states different areas that make some of their own laws

territories areas of the country outside the states

Torres Strait Islander someone who comes from this part of Queensland

tropical related to the tropics – the warmest parts of the world

Index

Titles in the *Destination Detectives* series include:

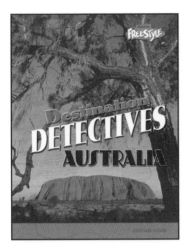

Hardback   1 406 20312 2

Hardback   1 406 20308 4

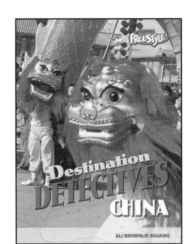

Hardback   1 406 20306 8

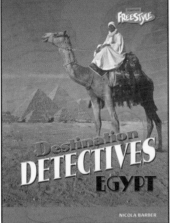

Hardback   1 406 20310 6

Hardback   1 406 20313 0

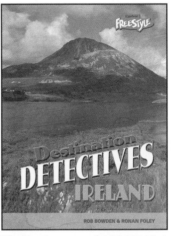

Hardback   1 406 20311 4

Hardback   1 406 20305 X

Hardback   1 406 20307 6

Hardback   1 406 20314 9

Find out about the other titles in this series on our website www.raintreepublishers.co.uk